# SNAKES AND REPTILES
## AROUND THE WORLD

A⁺

**Smart Apple Media**

Published by Smart Apple Media, an imprint of Black Rabbit Books
P.O. Box 3263, Mankato, Minnesota 56002
www.blackrabbitbooks.com

Library of Congress Cataloging-in-Publication Data

Alderton, David, 1956- author.
 Snakes and reptiles around the world / contributing authors, David Alderton [and nine others] ; consulting
editor, Per Christiansen.
     pages cm. -- (Animals around the world)
 Audience: Grades 4 to 6.
 Includes bibliographical references and index.
 ISBN 978-1-62588-197-7
1.  Reptiles--Juvenile literature.  I. Title.
 QL644.2.A43 2015
 597.9--dc23
                              2013043823

Contributing Authors: David Alderton, Susan Barraclough, Per Christiansen, Kieron Connolly,
Paula Hammond, Tom Jackson, Claudia Martin, Carl Mehling, Veronica Ross, Sarah Uttridge
Consulting Editor: Per Christiansen
Series Editor: Sarah Uttridge
Editorial Assistant: Kieron Connolly
Designer: Andrew Easton
Picture Research: Terry Forshaw

Printed in the United States at Corporate Graphics, Mankato, Minnesota
4-2014
PO 1650
9 8 7 6 5 4 3 2 1

# Contents

# Introduction

The class of reptiles includes a range of creatures such as snakes, lizards, turtles, crocodiles, iguanas, geckos, and many more. They have been around since the age of dinosaurs and can be found today all around the world. They are cold-blooded and have armored or scaly skin. They can be tiny or huge, ferocious, or timid.

# American Copperhead

The American copperhead will try to find a place where it can lie in wait for a mouse or a vole that it can ambush. But it also hunts and seeks out caterpillars. A young copperhead uses its brightly colored tail to attract a frog (that thinks the tail is a worm). It then eats the frog.

## WHERE DO THEY LIVE?

In northern Mexico and the southern and eastern US, from Texas to Massachusetts.

US

Mexico

## Camouflage

▶ If a human passes, the snake will freeze and, hidden in a heap of dead leaves, will be almost invisible.

## Venomous

◀ These snakes are venomous, but they are generally not aggressive. They will only usually bite if stepped on. The bites are painful to humans but not usually fatal.

## FACTS

**SIZE**

- Adults usually grow to 20–37 in. (50–95 cm).

- They have heat-sensitive pits below their eyes to find prey.

- Their venom destroys their prey's blood.

## DID YOU KNOW?

🖐 A young copperhead looks like an adult but is lighter in color and has a yellow tip on its tail.

🖐 Bites to humans can cause intense pain, tingling, throbbing, swelling, and nausea, and can also damage muscles and nerves.

🖐 When disturbed, a copperhead can produce a smell like cucumbers.

## Behavior

▶ In the southern United States, in the hot summer months, the copperhead is active at night. During the spring and fall, when it is cooler, it is active during the day. From October to February it returns to dens to hibernate. These dens may contain many snakes and will be used year after year.

# Anaconda

The anaconda is the most powerful of the giant snakes. It uses its massive coils to squeeze the life out of prey that seems too large to eat. The green anaconda is the largest snake in the world. It can be up to 24 ft. 9 in. (7.6 m) long. It stalks prey in the swamps and rivers of tropical South America. It feeds on fish or caimans and even jaguars and

## Huge Middle

▶ The anaconda is huge but it is the massive circumference of its middle, at nearly 3 ft. (1 m), that is most remarkable.

## WHERE DO THEY LIVE?

The tropical rain forests of South America and the swamp areas of Trinidad.

Trinidad

**South America**

## DID YOU KNOW?

 It can take weeks for an anaconda to digest one meal. It can live for months between meals.

It can stay underwater for as long as 10 minutes before it needs to come up for air.

 Its huge jaws are attached by stretchy ligaments that allow it to swallow its prey whole.

## Hunting

▶ An anaconda will hunt on land, but it prefers to stay in the water, where its huge body feels less bulky. To hunt, it lies at the surface of a stream or pond waiting for an animal to stop by for a drink or a rest. Its nostrils are on the top of its snout, so it can breathe while it is almost entirely under the water. Its teeth point backward, to help draw prey deeper into the snake's mouth.

## Oval Eyes

◀ The anaconda has no eyelids but its eyes are protected by a layer of skin called the brille. The oval-shaped pupil at the center of the eye helps it to see by night.

## FACTS

SIZE

- Moving on land, it leaves behind a deep, wide trench.

- The average size is 20 ft. (6.1 m).

- The female green anaconda is larger than the male.

# Bearded Dragon

This Australian lizard puffs out its throat pouch to reveal a "beard" of sharp-looking spines. It does this to scare off rivals or attackers. In fact, the spines are actually fairly soft and harmless. The bearded dragon bobs its head to show who's boss and waves its hands to show respect.

## Fireflies

▶ Bearded dragons cannot eat fireflies and other animals that produce light. This is because the light chemicals are poisonous.

## WHERE DO THEY LIVE?

**Australia**

The seven species of bearded dragon are found all across Australia.

## Good Eyesight

◄ It relies mainly on its excellent eyesight to find prey. Enlarged scales around the eyes help to keep out sand and dirt blowing in the semidesert landscape.

## FACTS

**SIZE**

● They grow to around 18–24 in. (45–60 cm) long.

● One-third of its total length is its tail.

● They live for five to six years.

## DID YOU KNOW?

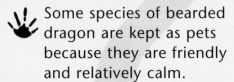

The legs of a bearded dragon are small but it can run extremely fast to escape from predators.

Some species of bearded dragon are kept as pets because they are friendly and relatively calm.

Males and females are about the same size, although males usually have a larger head.

## Feeding Time

▶ As omnivores, they eat both meat and plant matter. They mainly eat crickets, as well as leafy greens such as parsley and celery. They also eat fly larvae, locusts, silkworms, and flower greens, such as dandelion greens and rose petals. In captivity they will also eat non-citrus fruits such as strawberries.

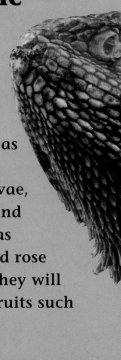

# European Adder

If a European adder finds a nest of mice or birds, it may eat the whole family. When two male adders fight over a female adder, they stick up their heads, wrap their bodies around each other, and try to push each other over. This is called the "dance of the adders" and can last 30 minutes.

## Sunshine

▶ When a European adder lies in the sun, it flattens its body as much as possible to expose its skin to the sun's heat.

## WHERE DO THEY LIVE?

They are found across northern Europe (except Ireland), and across Asia to northern China.

Europe

Asia

## Camouflage

◀ The adder has a dark zigzag pattern down its back. This hides it from enemies such as birds of prey by making the outline of the snake's body irregular.

## FACTS

SIZE

● Adults can grow to 35 in. (90 cm) in length.

● These snakes weigh between 2 and 6 oz. (50–180 g).

● European adders hibernate in winter.

## DID YOU KNOW?

🐾 The European adder and the common grass snake are the only snake species found inside the Arctic Circle.

🐾 The European adder is not aggressive and will only bite when stepped on or picked up.

🐾 If there is a hint of danger, it will usually disappear into the undergrowth.

## Snake Senses

▶ Its eyes have vertical slits for pupils in the center. This is usual in snakes that hunt at night, which the European adder does in the warmer parts of its range. Its strongest sense is its tongue. From this it can "taste" the air for prey. The male is usually gray and black; the female is brown.

# Gila Monster

The Gila monster's body is covered with bony, bead-like scales. Its bite can be very painful and is full of venom, which can kill reptiles, rodents, or rabbits. Male Gila monsters bite each other, but are immune to the venom. Strangely, the venom has little effect on frogs.

## Tough Armor

▶ Its scales do not overlap. They make a tough armor and help hold in moisture in the desert heat.

## WHERE DO THEY LIVE?

They are found in the southwestern USA and northwestern Mexico.

USA

Mexico

## Habitat

◀ They live in woodland, scrubland, and deserts that have some vegetation. They can climb trees and cacti in search of eggs.

## FACTS

**SIZE**

- They grow 16–22 in. (40–55 cm) long.
- They live for about 20 years in the wild.
- They weigh 10–12 lbs. (4–5 kg).

## DID YOU KNOW?

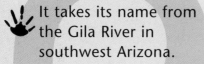 It takes its name from the Gila River in southwest Arizona.

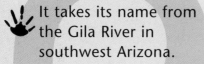 It has been known to live for three years without eating. In this time it survives off fat reserves in its tail.

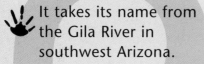 So many Gila monsters have been kept as exotic pets that they are now rare and protected by law.

## Eating and Hunting

▶ It is a heavy, slow-moving lizard and feeds on bird and reptile eggs, small birds, mammals, frogs, lizards, insects, and animals it finds that are already dead. It only eats five to ten times a year, but it might eat up to one-third of its weight when it does. It uses its strong sense of smell to find prey, even sniffing out and digging up buried eggs.

# Green Mamba

This swift, slim African snake spends most of its time high up in the trees. It is often found on plantations that grow mangoes, coconuts, and cashew nuts. It doesn't eat these, but it does eat the rats and birds that are attracted to the fruit.

## Head

▶ Behind the eyes are the venom glands. It has solid teeth in both jaws and two large venom fangs.

## WHERE DO THEY LIVE?

There are two species of green mamba. One lives in West Africa; the other lives in East Africa.

**Africa**

## Shedding Skin

◀ They need to shed their skin to grow, but do not have rocks to rub against. Instead, they snag their skin on twigs and slide out of their old skin.

## FACTS

SIZE

- It grows up to 8 ft. (2.5 m).

- It can live between 15 and 25 years in the wild.

- As a snake that hunts by day, it has round pupils in its eyes.

## DID YOU KNOW?

 It has enlarged belly scales that give the snake a good grip as it climbs tall tree trunks.

 Males compete for the attention of females by dancing with each other. Each male raises its head, threatening but not biting the other males in the dance.

 Untreated green mamba bites can kill humans.

## A Shy Snake

▶ Unlike its larger cousin the black mamba, the green mamba is shy. It would rather avoid contact with humans. It can move quickly—7 mph (11.3 km/h). If cornered, it might strike with its venomous fangs. It only hunts on the ground if prey cannot be found in trees.

# King Cobra

The heavy and muscular king cobra is the largest venomous snake in the world. It can kill other snakes with its powerful venom, and uses its menacing hood to warn off other animals. Just one bite from this highly poisonous snake is enough to bring down an elephant. The king cobra can grow to 18 ft. (5.5 m) long.

## WHERE DO THEY LIVE?

Widespread, but mainly in the rain forests and plains of India, southern China, and southeast Asia.

**Asia**

## DID YOU KNOW?

- It is the only snake in the world that builds a nest for its eggs.

- The king cobra is safe from the venom of its own kind. If one bites another, the venom has no effect.

- After one large meal, the king cobra can go for weeks without needing to eat again.

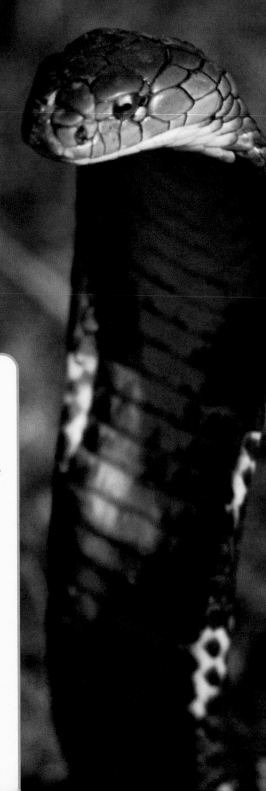

## Hood

▶ The cobra spreads its neck ribs to form the hood, which has false eyespots on it that may confuse or scare off predators.

## Threat Display

▶ It rears its head off the ground and spreads its neck into a "hood" to present a terrifying threat display toward intruders and predators. It preys on other snakes, even other venomous species. It overcomes them with its venom and then swallows them. The king cobra is a shy snake and will avoid people, but it can be very aggressive if it is cornered and feels threatened.

## Skin Color

◀ The skin is olive green, tan, or black, with faint, pale yellow cross-bands down the entire length of the body. The underbelly is cream or pale yellow.

**FACTS**

**SIZE**

● A single bite contains enough venom to kill 20 people.

● The fangs can grow to 0.5 in. (1.25 cm) long.

● Snake charmers in south Asia use king cobras in their acts.

# Komodo Dragon

The Komodo dragon is the heaviest and strongest lizard in the world. With a mouthful of sharklike teeth, powerful claws, and muscle-packed limbs, it can overpower animals much larger than itself. It eats by tearing off large chunks of flesh and swallowing them whole.

## Waterproof

▶ It is covered in a waterproof, scaly skin. This stops the dragon from drying out in the hot, tropical sunshine.

## WHERE DO THEY LIVE?

Komodo, Rinca, Gili Motang, and Flores, part of the Lesser Sunda Islands in Indonesia.

**Asia**

**Indonesia**

## Tongue

◀ The forked tongue is 12 in. (30 cm) long. It flicks out to "taste" the air for traces of prey animals. When resting, the tongue is drawn back into the head.

## FACTS

SIZE

- Komodo dragons are excellent swimmers.

- They hunt prey as big as water buffalos.

- They can live for 30 years or more.

## DID YOU KNOW?

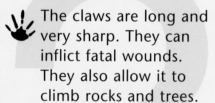 The claws are long and very sharp. They can inflict fatal wounds. They also allow it to climb rocks and trees.

It has an elastic stomach that can expand to hold a huge amount of food, allowing the dragon to cram its belly full.

A dragon's bite may contain at least four poisonous bacteria.

## Teeth

▶ The teeth of the Komodo dragon curve backward, helping the lizard grip struggling prey. The rear edges of the teeth are saw-edged like steak knives. New teeth replace old ones every three months, so the dragon always has a sharp set of butchering tools in its mouth.

# Marine Iguana

This unique black lizard spends much of its life shuffling between the baking rocks and the cold blue water. It is the only lizard that is fully adapted to marine life. It can stay underwater for long periods of time. It is also one of the few lizards that has a vegetarian diet.

## WHERE DO THEY LIVE?

On rocky coasts of the Galapagos Islands in the eastern Pacific.

Galapagos Islands

South America

## Scaly Skin

▶ The scaly skin is tough and waterproof to prevent injury and to keep it from drying out in the scorching sun.

## Feet and Toes

◀ The feet have strong toes and unusually long claws. This lets the marine iguana cling to rocks and so resist being swept away by the often powerful waves.

## FACTS

**SIZE**

- It might look fierce, but it is actually a gentle herbivore.

- All female iguanas are smaller than males.

- As the marine iguana grows, its skin continually peels away.

## DID YOU KNOW?

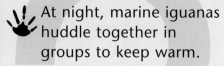 At night, marine iguanas huddle together in groups to keep warm.

The tail is flattened sideways. It is used like an oar to drive the iguana through the water.

It stops itself from overheating by sitting in shady areas or plunging into the cold sea.

## Crest and Nostril

▶ The marine iguana has a sawlike crest of horny spines along its back and tail, with longer spines on the nape of its neck. It has a special gland that opens into each nostril so the iguana can release unwanted salt from its system in a spray of salty water. The salt will often land on its head, giving it a distinctive white wig.

# Nile Crocodile

With its massive and powerful jaws, the Nile crocodile is a deadly threat to other creatures as it lurks beneath the water, waiting to snap them up. It is the largest reptile in Africa. It can grow up to 20 ft. (6 m) from snout to tail and weighs more than 1,984 lbs. (900 kg).

## WHERE DO THEY LIVE?

In Africa, south of the Sahara, along the River Nile, and in Madagascar.

**Africa**

**Madagascar**

## Teeth

▶ Its teeth grow continuously. After about two years, the worn-out teeth are forced out by the sharp new ones underneath.

## Fast Legs

◀ It walks with its legs splayed, but don't let the squashed look fool you: this animal can be fast. It has powerful feet and claws to climb up riverbanks.

## FACTS

● It can eat up to half its body weight in a single feeding.

● Up to 90 percent of Nile crocodiles die in their first year.

● It guards its nest until the eggs hatch.

SIZE

## DID YOU KNOW?

🖐 The Nile crocodile can stay underwater for more than an hour as it waits to ambush prey.

🖐 It is so powerful that it can drag a fully grown zebra underwater in just a few seconds.

🖐 All crocodiles have an acidic stomach so they can digest bones, horns, and hooves.

## Eyes and Nostrils

▶ The eyes sit above the head so that the crocodile can keep a lookout for prey while the rest of its body is under the water. The nostrils sit on a raised part of the snout. This allows the crocodile to breathe when the rest of its body is underwater. Flaps seal the nostrils to keep out water during dives. Clear "third eyelids" flick over to protect the eyes underwater.

# Rattlesnake

There are 32 species of rattlesnakes, and all of them are native to the Americas. They are predators and kill their prey with a venomous bite. The venom destroys body tissue and causes internal bleeding. Some rattlesnakes have a toxin that can paralyze. The rattle of the tail warns predators off, but hawks, weasels, and king snakes can kill rattlesnakes.

## Hearing

▶ They do not have ears on the outside of their bodies. Their hearing is weak, but they can feel vibrations in the ground.

## WHERE DO THEY LIVE?

They are found in the Americas, from southern Canada to central Argentina.

North America

Central America

South America

## Tongue

◀ They can smell with their nostrils and also with their tongues. The tongue carries the scent to an organ in the roof of the mouth, which identifies it.

## FACTS

**SIZE**

- They grow up to 6 ft., 6 in. (2.1 m) long.
- They weigh up to 12 lbs. (5 kg).
- In captivity, they can live for up to 30 years.

## DID YOU KNOW?

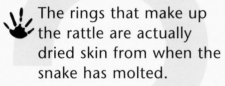 The rings that make up the rattle are actually dried skin from when the snake has molted.

The rattlesnake travels with its rattle held up to try to protect it from damage.

Its bite can be fatal to humans if not treated quickly, but a rattlesnake only bites if provoked.

## Looking for Prey

▶ Two pits, one in front of each eye, can sense heat over a short range of 1 ft. (0.3 m). The rattlesnake uses these to find and aim at prey. Each eye has a vertical slit pupil that opens wide in the dark to let in as much light as possible. It can see some colors but cannot see shapes very well. It relies on seeing movement.

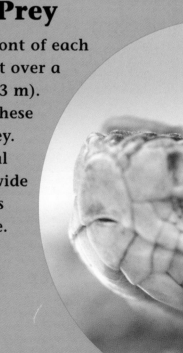

# Savannah Monitor

The main predators for the savannah monitor are snakes, birds, and people. It protects itself through camouflage. If threatened, it usually runs away or plays dead. But if cornered, it can defend itself by flicking its tail like a whip and by biting.

## Diet

▶ When young it feeds on millipedes and crickets. In adulthood it eats scorpions and frogs.

## WHERE DO THEY LIVE?

Africa

They live in West and Central Africa from Senegal to western Ethiopia.

## Attack

◀ When attacked, it can roll onto its back and hold its hind leg in its mouth, forming a ring. This makes it harder for a predator to swallow the monitor.

## FACTS

SIZE

- Adults are 3–5 ft. (1–1.5 m) long.
- They weigh 4–10 lbs. (2–4 kg).
- They can live up to 30 years.

## DID YOU KNOW?

🖐 In the wet season, its tail grows full of fat. It can live off this fat in the dry months.

🖐 Millipedes release a foul-tasting fluid to defend against monitors. But the monitor rubs them first with its chin, so that they release all their fluid. Only then does it snap them up.

## Thick Skin

▶ Its skin is very thick, so it keeps moisture inside and is not burned by the sun. This allows it to live in dry areas many miles from the nearest river or waterhole. However, it cannot survive for long in the real desert. Although it lives in such dry areas, it is a surprisingly good swimmer. Its skin is often sold for leather to make shoes, handbags, and watch straps.

# Glossary

**ambush** – to attack by surprise

**caimans** – small reptiles similar to crocodiles

**camouflage** – to conceal by blending in with the habitat

**captivity** – to be kept in enclosed area, such as a zoo, nature preserve, or as a pet.

**carnivore** – a meat-eating animal

**circumference** – distance around a circular object

**fatal** - deadly

**ferocious** – fierce and scary

**herbivore** – animal that only eats plants

**intruder** – an unwelcome outsider

**muscular** – having strong, powerful muscles

**molt** – to shed skin, feathers, or another outer layer periodically

**paralyze** – unable to move

**predator** – animal that lives by killing other animals

**prey** – animals that are killed by other animals

**reptile** – a cold-blooded animal such as snakes, lizards, and dinosaurs

**snout** – the large end of an animal's nose

**species** – a group of related animals that look like one another and can breed among themselves, but are not able to breed with members of another species.

**venom** – a poisonous matter

**vertical** - up-and-down direction

**Further Information:**

**Books**

**Hibbert, Clare.** *If You Were A Snake.* Smart Apple Media, 2014.

**Solway, Andrew.** *Snakes and Other Reptiles.* Heinemann Library, 2007.

**Simon, Seymour.** *Snakes.* HarperCollins Publishers, 2007.

**Squire, Ann O.** *Reptiles.* Scholastic, 2013.

**Taylor, Barbara.** *100 Things You Should Know About Snakes.* Mason Crest Publishers, 2010.

**Websites**

**http://www.http://www.bronxzoo.com/animals-and-exhibits/exhibits/world-of-reptiles.aspx**
The world of reptiles comes to life at the Brooklyn Zoo.

**http://www.livescience.com/27845-snakes.html**
Read all about fun facts about snakes

**http://www.nps.gov/ever/forkids/index.htm**
Discover the Everglades National Park

**http://animals.sandiegozoo.org/content/reptiles**
Learn all about reptiles from the San Diego Zoo

**http://www.sciencekids.co.nz/sciencefacts/animals/snake.html**
Fascinating trivia about snakes!

## Index: